The Powe

A Guide to Being a Happ...

Introduction

I want to thank you and congratulate you for purchasing the book, "The Power of Positivity."

This book contains proven steps and strategies on how to become happier and feel better.

It could be said that everything we do in our lives can traced back to the way our brains are working. The thoughts in our minds tend to reflect onto our bodies in the form of emotion. That emotion then has certain consequences to our lives. It affects our studies, our relationships, our choices – the list goes on. Hopefully this book can serve as an aid to understand the mind and to help it to become as positive as possible: for once our minds reach the fullest potential of positivity, then we can also reach our fullest potential.

Thanks again for purchasing this book, I hope you enjoy it!

Chapter 1 - *The Jubilant Brain*

When faced with life and what the day brings, your biggest support system is your brain. Without it, of course, nothing that you do would be possible. Brain functionality is altered by several factors, one of the biggest being your emotional state. Are you happy? Sad? Worried? Aloof? You have probably noticed that you get the most done when you are in a good mood. The tendencies to be productive are prominent and nothing seems too daunting to take on when you are feeling happy. This positivity not only helps with your responsibilities, but also with the way that you present yourself to others in your life. Maintaining healthy relationships with those around you is another essential component of keeping yourself stable. With these factors in line, your balanced mind will guide you towards making the best decisions.

Dopamine is your brain's best friend, an uplifting and motivational driving force behind your actions. Having the desire to be productive and accomplish goals feels great. While navigating through the daily tasks of life, the happiness that dopamine brings to your brain can assist you in many ways. From a psychological standpoint, it has been shown that happiness directly relates to your sense of well-being. If you are going through your day feeling secure and stable, your actions are most likely to mirror your mood. You will be able to effectively check items off of your to-do list with ease and be able to find a balance between your work and leisure time. Research has proven that doing good creates good. Showing gratitude in life activates your brain's receptors to dopamine and serotonin. In situations that are less than ideal, it is known that doing something selfless works to actually train your brain to be receptive to happiness and produce the chemicals that you need. This method works in very similar ways to antidepressants, which keep your brain happy and focused on positivity. (Barker, 2016)

Serotonin is an incredibly hard worker; it impacts every part of you, from your moods to the way that you function physically. With normal levels of serotonin, you should feel calmer, balanced, and happier. This partnership between dopamine and serotonin is essential for you to feel your best. If one or both are lacking, you may start to feel anxious and unable to sleep at night. Though some are born with chemical imbalances, when possible, doing things to keep your levels up can provide you with a much happier way of living. You will feel that you are able to take on your days with ease, and you will be able to stay focused and emotionally grounded along the way. A simple step to activate these receptors is by going outside. Sunlight is a great source of natural healing when you are seeking a little bit more serotonin. Eating a healthy diet is also very beneficial. There are certain foods that you can incorporate into your diet to give an additional boost of serotonin. (Bergland, 2012)

A counterpart to your dopamine and serotonin levels are the infamous endorphins that are naturally produced by your body. These natural chemicals interact with the receptors in your brain and provide you with an uplifted mood, a natural high. There are many ways for you to organically improve the production of endorphins. When you exercise regularly, this is one way that you are helping yourself both physically and mentally. This release of endorphins further protects you from anxiety, depression, insomnia, and even addictions. With this positive release of chemicals, staying optimistic and energetic in life becomes second nature. It is often overlooked, but another way to release more endorphins is to laugh more! Watching a funny movie or sharing humorous memories with friends will provide you with a much-needed rush of endorphins. Consuming yourself into a new hobby can also prove to be highly beneficial. Each step of the way, when you begin to recognize the progress that you are making in your newfound craft, you will feel a sensation of desire to accomplish even more. This can further trigger an endorphin rush and assist you in being the happiest person that you can be. (Axe, 2017)

It may seem like a no-brainer to most, but it is very important to maximize your happiness whenever possible. We often put ourselves on the back burner simply because we forget to factor our mental health into the equation in the first place! By taking care of yourself, you will notice a huge increase in productivity. Self-care is just as important as taking care of a loved one. As people, we need love and nurturing to grow, and this includes the way that we treat ourselves. If you have ever found yourself to be in a "slump," then you know the feeling of defeat. Accomplishing even the simplest tasks can feel like a chore when you are unhappy. It is important to acknowledge how you are feeling, even during the worst times. Recognizing that you are unhappy takes away the power behind it. Your next step is actualizing happiness— how are you going to accomplish this? Think about something that you can do to change your predicament, something that you can implement immediately. Work on some goals, both long term and very short term. Giving yourself something to look forward to, no matter how minor, could be the jumpstart that your brain needs to get back on track. As soon as you are able to become productive, it is like a domino effect of happiness to come.

The way that you wake up in the morning is a good indication of how your day is going to unfold. Simply setting aside a few moments to think positively can highly improve the quality of your day, and in turn, your life. Putting out good intentions before you even get out of bed is going to draw in positive energy that you can utilize during the times in your day when you need it most. Thinking positively does not mean thinking unrealistically. It is important to remember that no matter how happy and stable you are, there are always going to be moments that test your strength and your patience. Channeling these uplifting emotions can be used as a tool when you need a pick me up. The same idea applies to the thoughts that you have before you go to sleep at night. No matter what you went through during the day, it is important to not hold onto any stressors because they can be harmful to your psyche. Again, channeling your positivity has been known to improve your days and even provide you with a more restful night's sleep. The more familiar that you become with positive thinking, the more you can weave it into your life.

By embarking on a more positive lifestyle, you will notice a chain reaction of changes that will take place, not only within yourself, but also with others around you. When you emit happiness, you may notice the magnetic effect that it will have, improving your relationships and friendships. You will notice that your positive spirits will attract like-minded people into your life. Being able to talk to someone with a pleasant demeanor is much more enjoyable than talking to someone who is constantly blaming their circumstances for their misfortunes. Not only will you start to feel great about yourself, but you will also influence others to take on a more positive role in their own lives. Communication becomes easier, and this can improve your connections to people. In most cases, the number one cause of conflict is due to miscommunication and misunderstanding. The ability to clearly and confidently express yourself correlates directly to your happiness.

It is proven that most people who choose to spend time with family, friends, and significant others on a regular basis are happier than those who do not. The ability to share your thoughts and feelings with another person keeps your stress levels down and feelings of depression at bay. A healthy relationship, whether it be platonic or intimate, involves a mutual exchange of caring and communication. Even by listening to someone else's problems and providing positive encouragement, you will find that this can also positively impact your own state of mind. In addition, this will strengthen the bond of your relationship, allowing you to feel closer to the person that you are talking to. By successfully maintaining relationships in your life, when anything goes wrong, you will feel that sense of having a support system. This is important because often times, when negativity starts to occur is when you are most likely to feel alone. (Wallis, 2005)

Being able to achieve long term goals also goes hand-in-hand with happiness. It is said that once we create a goal in our minds, our subconscious never forgets it. Through various distractions and changes in your life, the goal remains. This proves that no matter how much time has lapsed, it is not too late to pursue something that you have always wanted to do. At any point in time, you have the ability to completely change the direction that your life is going. You can move to a new city, get a different job, and date someone you have not met yet. Getting out of a rut is entirely possible and will renew your sense of passion for life. Just because you may have tried something in the past that did not work out does not mean that you can't try it again. Humans are generally success-oriented; we like feeling accomplishment and getting recognition for our achievements. Having goals gives you a greater sense of purpose, which in turn, gives you the drive and motivation to succeed. Overall, it is clear to see how this can directly impact your state of happiness. (Hacheyart, 2012)

Because your quality of life will improve by being happy, so will the length of it. Long term studies have shown that this is true; there is a clear connection between your mood and your health. Individuals who are able to remain happy are known to live longer. Happiness also correlates to a clean bill of health. The stressors that tend to linger from pessimism are abolished, and in time, you will develop immunity to these things. You are also less likely to suffer from illness and disease that stem from a negative outlook when you are enforcing positivity in your life. Although, there is no guarantee that you will fully be able to avoid these health concerns 100% of the time, choosing a happy lifestyle lowers your odds of having poor health by a landslide. (Yates, 2011)

Chapter 2 - Meditation and Mindfulness

Our thoughts reflect onto our bodies and create emotions. After knowing this, the next logical step is to become as aware of our thoughts as possible. Once we shine the light of awareness over our thinking, it's emotional power dissipates. For example, imagine you get into a fight with your significant other. Even when the fight is over, swirling memories and thoughts can pop back up and destroy your mood. When this happens, simply notice that you are getting lost in those thoughts and accept it. Then it is a matter of staying aware of your thoughts until that energy fades and your emotions go back to normal – a ball thrown up into the air will come back down if it is not fed anymore energy. Of course, it is always easier said than done!

Meditation is ultimately one of the most beneficial and simple ways that you can take your desire for happiness to the next level. The reason is that meditation clears the mind and allows you to see unhealthy thought patterns; becoming aware of those patterns can help greatly. There are several ways to meditate, and there is no such thing as a right way or a wrong way. Sitting alone for 5-10 minutes in a quiet room and focusing your thoughts qualifies as meditation. There are many resources available in the form of books, CDs, and even videos online that give you a guided meditation experience with positive words and calming music from home. For a more social experience, most yoga studios and spiritual healing centers offer meditation classes. In these classes, a group of people meditate together and collectively channel their positive energy towards good intentions for all. Having a clear mind improves your ability to hold onto your happiness and focus your energy on positive and productive things.

Perhaps the simplest way to start meditating is to simply sit with the eyes clothes. Sit with your spine erect so that you are alert. Begin breathing in and out while observing each breath. Observation of your focus is the foundation of meditation and as you practice, you will soon find that your focus keeps increasing in anything that you do. Thoughts will come, but just allow them while observing them. Let them pass and refocus on the breath.

You can start at doing 10 minutes daily, eventually increasing to 20 minutes daily and beyond. The important thing is to make it a habit – do it every day. It is much better to meditate most days of the week for 10 minutes than to meditate for one day of the week for an hour. Try not to burn yourself out and just take it slow. It is a practice like anything else in life: keep working at it and give yourself time to grow.

Another way to meditate is with mantras. Instead of keeping your focus on your breath, you can keep your focus on mentally saying a syllable, word, or phrase. Let's use the syllable "Om" for this example. As before, thoughts will arise, but as they do, let them go and refocus on the "Om." As time goes on, it will seem more like you are listening to the "Om" instead of actually saying it in the mind. The "Om" may change form but just allow it and observe it. The deeper you go, the closer you are to the source of all thoughts. This can be helpful in changing the context many people see as life – it can be realized that life is more than just the way that thoughts affect perceptions.

Breathing is another important aspect. The depth of breath can have a surprising effect on mental state. Have you ever been in an anxious situation and had someone tell you to take deep breathes? It no doubt works, but why not just practice breathing more deeply at all times? Deep breathing (and meditation as well) is something that should be taught to children at an early age, and possibly in school, in my opinion. The deeper and longer you breathe translates to a deeper sense of calm in the mind. It is easy to get lost in the swing of life and forget your breathing, but is it definitely worth it. The best thing about deep breathing is it is free! Oxygen has no price tag.

While you are meditating and focused on your breath, you can take a break and focus on gratitude for a little bit and see how it makes you feel. No matter how much life has beaten you up, there is always something to be grateful for. Whatever you focus on becomes your reality. Focusing on these things for some time can lead to positive feelings. It can also balance out your perspective – no one should get too negative!

Meditating seated with the eyes closed might be the easiest. This is due to the fact that when you become lost in thought, you eventually will remember that you are sitting with the purpose of meditation, but there is also value in meditating in everyday life. This can be called mindfulness. As written about above, what we focus on becomes our perceptions. As we go about our everyday life, doing chores, doing work, going to school, try to focus on and observe everything that we do and think about. That way we become more of an observer and less of a participant, and we then get more control over our thoughts and emotions.

Meditation, breathing, and remembering where we place our focus can be daunting especially at the beginning.

The key thing is to practice. Anything that you do many times you will become better at. Keep some patience for yourself and don't get burned out all at once. As you make progress reward yourself and try to enjoy the journey. Training mindfulness is like going to the gym except for the brain, except instead of getting stronger muscles, we can get a stronger focus and awareness, and ultimately more peace.

Chapter 3 - Imagination

From a very young age, children can use their creativity to create an imagined alternative to reality. Why not put this to good use in increasing positivity? Very often, we put proverbial chains on ourselves. We tell ourselves: I don't deserve to be happy, or, I only deserve to be this amount of happy. Well, why not tell ourselves the opposite?

Even though many of us have not taken drama classes, we can still practice role-playing. Imagine that you are the happiest person in the universe. What is stopping you from feeling like the happiest person? Nothing. Allow yourself to be happy and remember even in trying times that nothing is forcing you to not be happy. Perhaps through natural selection, we are conditioned to always desire and to never be full. Even though that may be the case, we have still developed the mental capacity to accept the way things are and to be happy with it in many cases.

Practice role-play and the use of imagination positively. There is no natural rule saying that we must only be happy in certain circumstances. You may be surprised at some the contexts in which you can pull happiness out of yourself where you previously thought it is impossible. With the human mind and imagination, nothing is impossible.

Chapter 4 - Thought Classification

The power of thinking has a great impact on the way that we function. Thinking reflects onto the body in the form of emotion. It is perfectly normal to have days full of doubt. Life is not a one way street; it is normal to feel in over your head at times. On those low days, it is important to remember that often times the mind can be too powerful. Overthinking a problem will result in an overworked mind. Negative thoughts will start to pop into your head, so what can be done to combat them? There is no need to suppress these thoughts because they are appearing for a reason. However, if you are able to keep them separate from your emotions, sorting through these feelings will come with ease. Start by determining where the thought is coming from. Is it stemming from something going on in your life? Has a friend done something to upset you and put you in a bad mood? Did you not get the promotion that you were banking on? Whatever the reason may be, accept it and let it be. Allow yourself these thoughts, but end it there. By keeping them as thoughts and not letting them develop into emotions, the negative feelings will eventually subside. It is a bit like throwing a ball. At first there is energy in the ball, but with time the energy fades and the ball falls back to the ground.

As with most self-improvement, convincing yourself to let go of anger and sadness is not the easiest thing to do. When you are stuck in your negative rut of emotions, it is almost as if they begin to multiply in your brain. Remembering to breathe is where you need to begin. Try to make your breathing the priority and inhale deeply for 5 seconds while continuing to exhale for 5 seconds. Doing this for a few minutes will restart the brain and allow you to regroup your thoughts. Once your mind begins to clear, think to yourself about why exactly you are feeling this way. What is the first thing that comes to mind? Write this down and continue to journal until you fill up a page about this stressor. Allowing yourself to free write and use word association can provide more insight into your problems that you may not have realized before. If you still feel unhappy after you've done this, think about what you can do to make a change. Does the next step involve talking to someone? Do you need a nice day with your best friend to take your mind off of things? You will know what feels right.

So what do you do with all of the emotions that are already built up inside of you? Let them out and let them go. Clearing the clutter of your mind will ultimately help you on your way to happiness. If you want to express your happiness, allow yourself to do this. The same goes for any negative emotions that you may come across. Think of your emotions as secondary to your feelings, because they are temporary. If you keep your emotions bottled up inside, you are much more likely to have a breakdown, possibly snap at someone who hasn't done anything wrong but who wants to know if you are okay. Losing your temper when you are suppressing emotions is very common because it can build up very easily; this quickly transforms into the feeling of instability. In your mind, lashing out might feel justified, almost a much needed release. To those around you who are not feeling the same emotions, it might make a little bit less sense. Using healthy methods to expel your emotions will leave you feeling like you have more clarity, and those around you will also have a much better understanding of what you are going through.

Coping with negative emotions in a productive way will allow you to get them out of your head and also allow you to move forward. Perhaps you have a short fuse because you feel that you are over-worked, over-stressed. A healthy way to cope can be achieved through relaxation. Treat yourself to a massage or a spa day once a month. This will give you something to look forward to and keep your emotions in check. Another way to desensitize yourself is by changing up your environment. Go for a hike on a trail you've never visited before. Choose to see a movie in an unfamiliar but nearby town. Getting yourself out of your normal routine is a great way to break up negative emotions that may start to form. If you feel that you just can't manage these emotions on your own, talk to a therapist. The stigma around seeing a professional for help us unfortunate because most people could benefit from it. There is nothing wrong with asking for help, and it actually illustrates how strong you are by acknowledging that you need this help. Therapy isn't for everyone, but if you feel that you need to give it a try, your intuition is probably leading you down the correct path. These ways to cope will work differently for each individual, so don't be discouraged if you try one and it doesn't work for you. Keeping an open mind and not limiting yourself will help you with your own coping strategy.

A mistake that is commonly made is when people allow their doubtful thoughts to take over their lives. These thoughts can deter you from trying new things in fear that you will fail, or even being too overwhelmed to embark on familiar activities. When you are doing this regularly, it is almost like psyching yourself out. It is parallel to the saying of being afraid of striking out before even playing the game—thoughts that manifest themselves into negative emotions can hinder you. Being held back by your own negativity is unhealthy. This is why the idea of compartmentalization can help you.

This is the process of organizing your thoughts but not giving them additional meanings or expectations. Being able to correctly identify and categorize your thoughts will allow you to see the problems in your life as a bigger picture rather than a road block. All that seems devastating to you in the moment may not necessarily feel the same in a month, even a week, from now. As people, we have the ability to adapt to any given situation or any changes that may occur. Some of us find this easier than others, but with the correct mental training, it is possible to learn how to become more flexible to change.

We often confuse certain emotions as accurate predictions of how situations are going to unfold. For example, not wanting to approach someone new due to a lingering (yet unjustified) suspicion that they are not going to like you. Emotions are based on the way that you are feeling, and while that is perfectly valid in the moment, it may not always necessarily be the most accurate representation of the truth. Given the situation above, perhaps the other person wants to talk to you just as much, but is feeling the same nervous emotions and is also discouraged from making the first move. Putting yourself out there, expressing true vulnerability, is a wonderful trait that sometimes must be mastered over time. There is usually not reward without risk. If you realize that you want to talk to someone or to partake in something, act before your mind has the chance to react. Opening yourself up to new opportunities, or things that make you feel nervous, excited, sensitive, or all of the above, will help you grow as a person. In this growth, you will be able to learn a lot about yourself and realize which aspects make you the happiest.

An important lesson to remember is to listen to your emotions, but to not let them rule you. Allowing yourself to be taken over by any one thing is not fair, but feeling an emotion and letting yourself reflect on it is ideal. The same way that is it unhealthy to indulge in an entire cake in one sitting, being consumed in an emotion can also yield unhealthy results. Your judgement becomes foggy and you start to experience tunnel vision when making decisions that are solely based on emotions. Allow yourself to feel happy, to feel scared, to feel excited, to feel angry, but recognize that the feeling is fleeting and only a part of who you are as an entire being. You are so much more than these feelings, so don't let yourself be amounted to anything less. When you are able to balance your emotions, you'll start to use them more as a contemplative tool rather than an interference. Working in this harmony, you will notice that this aligns with your desire for balance and happiness in life.

Curiosity often gets the best of us, and this is normal considering that there is much left unknown when it comes to interacting with other people. Keeping your own emotions in check is great, but you can't necessarily predict what another person is going to say and how they are going to react. The benefit of socializing is the unknown, not knowing what the other person is going through in the moment or how they are feeling deep down. Honest and organic interaction stems from this mystery place, curiosity keeping the conversation alive. Before you allow any negativity to creep into your mind, consider that your viewpoint of a person or situation is very limited. Allow room for acceptance and understanding, because you would ask for the same. Your thoughts stem from your outward observations, which are finite. Training yourself to have an open mind in these situations and refraining from swaying your judgement is key. You will become a more understanding person and you will also begin to be more forgiving and understanding with yourself.

When witnessing this internalization of negative energy in others, it can be easy to form a judgement and even a dislike. Those who choose to live negatively attract negativity. Having an attitude that the world is out to get you will leave you feeling permanently negative and almost anticipating what bad thing is going to happen next. If you have ever met a person and felt this bad energy, consider that maybe they are unaware of what they are expelling. Learning more about living a positive and happy life will help you when you encounter people who are simply stuck in their own ways. We all make choices in our lives to act certain ways, so instead of trying to change people, all that you are able to do is accept them. By doing this, you will feel at peace knowing that you have no "enemies." Because even if the other person is the problem, this still creates bad energy that you will carry around. You may notice that by taking this neutral stance and not letting negativity affect you, others may be drawn to you in the way of serving an inspiration or a source of sound advice. Leading by example is the most beneficial way to help someone who is struggling but not exactly asking you for help. Our environment and others around us serve as factors in the way that we live our lives.

The law of attraction is another wonder of the social world. When you are pursuing a new relationship with someone, this is often a time when your emotions could interfere. Naturally, the expectations are greater when romantic feelings are involved. Jealousy issues stem from these expectations, as well as many other downfalls. So, whether you are in a long-term relationship already, or simply pursuing a new one, the ways that you teach yourself to cope with your emotions can help you. Learning how to take emotional cues and not simply explode with an overreaction will keep your relationships healthy. Arguments are inevitable, the opportunity to disagree when you are becoming so close to someone. Take this in stride and remember to use your best judgement with your clearest mind. It is impossible to truly resolve an issue when you do not even understand the root of the problem. As you do with your own internal struggles, evaluate any argument or disagreement that you have and think to yourself what you intend on doing about it. In most cases, both people are working towards the same goal of resolution but are just too stubborn to realize it. We all want to be acknowledged, and this is why the importance of clear communication is essential.

A positive balance is created when you can inhale positivity and exhale all that is negative. Like a flower in bloom, you as a person also have the opportunity to blossom and grow. Not only is negative thinking harmful to yourself, but others will also be impacted by it. Most of us are uncomfortable in situations that involve confrontation. Once you practice keeping your emotions in check, this becomes much easier to face. Being able to let go of confrontation, of your bad days, and of stressful situations will help you become a better-rounded person. This doesn't mean that you need to pretend all is well when it isn't. Allow yourself to recognize when something is negative, not in your favor, but avoid the internalization of that energy. Instead, channel your energy into a solution to the problem. Ask yourself—what am I going to do next to improve this situation? You'll find that by taking this simple step towards positive thinking, you will not feel as burdened in hard situations. The more that you choose balanced ways over being controlled by negativity, the more you will start to form a healthy habit that impacts every aspect of your life.

Chapter 5 - Trusting Your Mind

Learn how to become your own personal cheerleader. Don't sit on the sidelines in your own life—keep singing those praises, because you will benefit from this confidence boost! There is a great impact that comes from believing in yourself and encouraging yourself, and there is no reason to deny this positivity. Whether you are doing something important or simply getting through another day, it is important to have that self-recognition. Allow yourself to feel proud and build yourself up when you can. You will realize that having confidence is not self-indulgent, but it will actually help to bring good things into your life. Dispel any thoughts that discourage you from being kind to yourself. Having a mantra of self-love is one of the most positive but hardest steps you can take on your search for happiness. It is no secret that we are often our own toughest critics. So why is it so much easier to judge ourselves than to judge others? This ties in with understanding emotions. Thoughts are constantly going through your mind, and if you get into the habit of holding onto the bad ones, you might start to blame yourself for things or deny yourself praise when you deserve it. Learning to use positive language when you are addressing yourself is a simple step in being your own support system.

Eliminate the word "can't" from your vocabulary entirely. The moment you decide that you cannot do something, your mind will hold onto that mentality. When something seems impossible, take a moment to find out where the source of your doubt is coming from. Are you yearning to visit a new country but feel that you can't because of your financial state? Don't rule this out! Instead, think about how you might not be able to take a trip in the moment, but you are still able to brainstorm ways to make it happen in the future. Think about your saving and spending habits; make a plan of action. People who live proactively are able to accomplish more than those who discourage themselves and shut down thoughts or ideas from the start. If you continue to choose methods that ultimately discourage you, you may be reluctant to try new things or accomplish your goals. This takes a lot of mental focus, not only to implement, but also to acknowledge. As you go through your day, think about how many times you tell yourself that you can't do something. The amount of circumstances may surprise you. Challenge yourself to think outside of the box, to reach further than you are currently reaching.

Expand your thinking to realize that you are capable of more than you are aware of. When things are going well in your life and you feel content, you might decide that you are going to remain stagnant. This creates a sense of security, but ultimately, you will become a self-fulfilling prophecy. By stopping when you get over one hurdle in life, you are not allowing yourself to progress. Those who are doing well in life, yet still feel unsatisfied, are potentially getting themselves into a rut without realizing it. Depression can sneak in when you least expect it, even when things in life don't necessarily seem terrible. If you have ever felt this way, perhaps it is because you are putting limits on yourself. It can be hard to determine what steps to take next when things are going well. Your fight or flight response will not be activated, so instead, you will need to look around yourself. Perhaps gain some inspiration from a friend, relative, or even a stranger. By keeping your eyes open to these things, you may realize new goals that you want to accomplish that you had never thought about before.

Writing down your goals, dreams, aspirations, and wishes will remind you that there is more that you are capable of. Keeping these thoughts flowing will actually begin to impact how you live your day to day life. You will realize that you will take more chances and push yourself a little bit more. With a goal in mind, this gives you the motivation and drive that is needed in life to keep going. Surrounding yourself with other goal-oriented people is going to boost this progress as you head toward your goals. Talk about them frequently! If you have people in your life that you can bounce ideas off of and report your progress to, you will be able to remain driven. To keep things organized, make lists. Use categories to determine what you want in the present, the near future, and the future that exists in the years to come. These lists will become a rough draft of what you wish to accomplish. When you need a reminder of reasons why you should push yourself harder, turn to your lists. Not everybody needs to create a solid life plan to stick to though; life is unpredictable, and it is okay to deviate from the plan! Think of yourself as a work in progress, flexible to change and easily adaptable to whatever life throws your way.

In a physical sense, your appearance ties in greatly to your self-belief. Keep up with your hygiene and take care of your body. Eliminate excessive use of chemicals and substances that can weigh you down and even make you feel sluggish and depressed. Certain foods that are heavily processed and contain artificial preservatives can actually impact your happiness and overall physical health. The way you dress also comes into play—wear clothing that you feel comfortable in, but also is appropriate for the situation at hand. You'll realize that if someone appears to be well-groomed and put together outwardly, we take them more seriously and may even express admiration towards them.

Always allow yourself a decent amount of sleep no matter how hectic your life may become. Sleep is meant to rejuvenate your body, mind, and energy. Let yourself rest, but keep it balanced. Too much rest can also cause less than favorable results. Without your working body, your mind would be much less impactful.

In learning about yourself on a deeper level, you are probably going to experience insecurity and discomfort. You may want to shut down or resist constructive criticism. This is natural and expected, because we often only skim the surface of ourselves. By diving deeper and accepting that what makes you uncomfortable, not only will you get to know yourself better, but you will also be able to determine your strengths and weaknesses. Again, balance is key—do not focus on any one strength or any one weakness for too long. Actively working on balancing the two is how you will strengthen the weak. Character building happens every single day, and it would be unfair to limit ourselves by objectifying our traits. Look at yourself as a human being and not only a piece of the puzzle. As you begin to learn more about yourself, you will also be able to learn which ways motivate you the best. Some of us are visual learners, others respond best to sound. Utilize your most responsive senses, and watch your self-confidence grow.

Setting forth into something unfamiliar or even most familiar may result in the unknown. This is not a negative or harmful result, and it is important that you train yourself to accept that not everything is black and white. If you knew all the answers, there would be no opportunity to grow. Taking these chances will build up that thick skin needed for those times when your voice shakes. Being scared and nervous is natural, and it is possible to handle these times with a positive influence. In any situation, remember to breathe. This will make sure you are centered as you approach the situation. Breath control plays an active role in achieving positive thinking. Look at the situation as if you are bigger than it; this will give you strength and avoid stressful feelings. With this mentality, truly anything is possible. It is never wrong to tell yourself that you are amazing and that you can accomplish anything.

Having faith in yourself is like switching on a magnetic pull that attracts happiness. There are many ways in which you can train your thoughts to become more supportive and accepting of yourself. The more you practice these positive tactics, the more successful you will become. Like most things, repetition is key. While repeating these steps, you will create a helpful habit that will make it as easy as possible to release this self-love. If you take a look at the most successful people you can think of, you will probably realize that they are extremely driven and self-sufficient. Think about the driving force behind their actions, that fire that is lit underneath them. Much inspiration can be found in successful people who have what you seek to accomplish. At the end of the day, you are the one who has to live with your choices and actions. It is considered a success if you are able to feel happy about the person that you are. If you don't like something, change it! Having harmony with yourself will result in you feeling happier and well-rounded—the ultimate goal. It is amazing the impact that living life with positive intentions can have on a person.

Chapter 6 - Rich in Resources

When presented with a situation, whether we are aware of it or not, our brains silently evaluate the outcome. This judgement remains in our subconscious, sometimes spilling forward if we are feeling stimulated by the result (nervous, scared, excited, blissful, etc. . .). Although this is often happening below the surface of what our mind can control, it is in good practice to try and look at things with a glass half full mentality. This saying is probably not new to you, as a lot of people either see situations in one of two ways—glass half full or glass half empty. Just like the other positive habits that we try to take on, viewing the outcome of things with a positive mentality is going to be beneficial to you. Training yourself to put your pessimism at bay will allow for this glass half full mentality to become your go-to. The way that we first perceive things is an indicator of how they are going to make us feel, think, and act. Like with any structure, starting from the foundation or root is going to give you the most solid beginning.

A fun way to determine how you are perceiving life is to take a few of the notable moments of your day and to think about the results they have yielded; were these positive or negative? How did you handle them? Try to remove yourself from the situation and look at it as if you were watching a character in a movie or a novel. By distancing yourself, you will be able to see the full impact of these choices. Would you have done anything differently? Make a mental note, and if the situation arises again, try it! This is yet another form of self-evaluation that will lead you to a better understanding. When it comes to life, we function on trial and error. It is okay to experiment with our choices and actions. As you learn more about yourself, you will want to focus on solutions instead of problems. Thinking about potential opportunities will fill your brain with positive encouragement in the future rather than spending too much time dwelling on what you should have done.

Once feelings are mastered, move on to decision making. The process of making a clear choice will become easier once you have pinpointed your feelings towards something. When you need to make a choice, you will likely think about how the result will impact you. Broaden this perspective to consider how this will affect others around you and any other factors involved. Sometimes, the best decision is not always the clearest. Do you reach for the choices that provide you with instant gratification? While this may seem like the best solution at the time, expand your thinking to include any future impact that this may have. Good things are always worth the wait, and having control of your patience and understanding will assist you in making decisions. By doing this, you will become a more well-rounded and positive person. If you need to, weigh out the pros and cons. This will give you tangible knowledge about the situation at hand, allowing you to make a clear decision. With most things, it is often said to go with your gut, so don't let yourself overthink it. Once you've made a choice, act on it and don't look back with regret. The power of positive choices teaches you how to move forward.

Let your actions speak louder than your words. As it has been echoed, be your biggest support system. Stand by yourself and the decisions that you make, and allow room for mistakes. Being able to admit when you are wrong is an admirable trait, another one that might need to be taught as a habit. This all ties in with being completely honest. If you are able to admit your faults, then you will be able to learn and grown from them. Being able to see errors in your actions comes from the acceptance of the responsibility of the situation. This trait is not a sign of weakness, and it will help you in any circumstance. This is also a reflection of your integrity. When you are able to admit that you are wrong, others will see that you have those strong ethics.

Perhaps you have seen the difficulty in being around highly defensive people. All forms of defense mechanisms are basically forms of dishonesty to the self and to others. The psychoanalyst Sigmund Freud first spoke about mental defense mechanisms. Denial when a person flat out claims something happened a certain way when in reality it didn't. There is projection when someone pushes out their qualities onto others while denying them in themselves. There is rationalization when someone makes excuses for choices or mistakes that happen. It can be observed that people who carry these defense mechanisms do not grow as much as they potentially could. They are missing out on the intense value that exists in self-honesty and the growth that can come afterwards. All humans make mistakes, but you can only grow from them and become better once the mistakes are acknowledged.

Human shame is a negative emotion that can totally drain positivity. The answer to dealing with shame is to take responsibility for your mistakes and accept them. This means being totally honest about what happen and admitting that it was a dumb move. The next step is to take accountability to be better in the future. If a person does not truly take accountability to become better in the future, there will no doubt be a decrease in trust in that person. If you truly regret a mistake, that is okay, everyone is human, but you absolutely must not do it again. Responsibility and then accountability for the future is the best way to handle mistakes.

While the past has the ability to shape the person that you are today, don't let it hold you back. We have all experienced things that have hindered us, and possibly even changed us. While it can be easy to dwell on them, or even hold them accountable for our daily actions, it is not the smartest approach to take. Our past should be a tool that gives us perspective, not a scapegoat for our present-day actions. If you spend your time blaming your past for situations in the present, you will not be able to move on. Accepting and ultimately letting go of your past is a step that must be taken on your journey of self-love. When you are able to do this, you will find it easier to live a happy life.

We are fed different ideals of how we are supposed think and act; decide for yourself. Comparing and contrasting is a good way to see what areas of yourself that you can improve on. Don't lose your identity, though! While this comparison can be informative and highlight the ways you can change, remember to stay true to who you are. Becoming a carbon copy of someone else isn't realistic to living your own life. Just because another person might be on a different stepping stone than you, this does not mean that you won't get there in your own time while utilizing your own methods. When choosing who you spend your time with, make mental notes of how they support and encourage you. Sometimes, jealousy plays a role in friendships, and your friends might be putting you down. Just as it is important to choose a healthy intimate relationship if you are involved with someone, it is also just as important to choose healthy friendships. Be around people who want to build you up and encourage your success.

In the media, we are also given opportunities to compare ourselves to those in the spotlight. This can become very damaging to the psyche, because we only see a fraction of these people's lives. Celebrities are able to project their successes for the world to see, and it is natural that we may become influenced by this. A lot of what celebrities do becomes glamorized by the media, and this can start to impact you without you even realizing it. Keeping yourself balanced and grounded is essential. When you are sure of yourself as a person, you will have the confidence to see what others are doing (even the rich and famous) while still feeling proud of yourself and your own personal achievements. It is not wrong if you would like to gather inspiration from public figures to help better yourself, but do this in ways that are appropriate for you own life.

As you get to know yourself better, and you learn how to utilize the inspiration around you, you'll realize what your reality is. Adjusting your expectations is important. Having goals is a great motivational force, and making sure your expectations are not set too high or too low will help you achieve them. You will find that you gain much more satisfaction when you accomplish these realistic goals. To help you in this, create a plan. The brainstorming is worth it, because you will be able to pinpoint what you want out of life. Once you have a couple of ideas, place these goals on a timeline. You can make this as short term or as long term as you wish. This is not meant to put too much pressure on you, but to keep reminding you of what you are aiming for. As you are working on accomplishing these goals, don't forget to track your progress! It is often easy to forget how far you have come unless you take a moment to reflect on it. Recognize that you are trying your best, and you will stay motivated. It is also great to reward yourself along the way. You deserve to be treated as you reach your milestones!

Another freeing, positive trait—the ability to move past any transgressions of the past. Forgiveness of actions is important, both towards others and towards yourself. Whether it be a simple personality clash or a moral debate, it is perfectly normal to feel hostility in some cases. Those who live positive, happy lives handle this disconnect by their ability to let go. In order to accomplish this, you will need to make the conscious choice that you would like to let go of the issue. In making this decision, this does not mean that you are going to suppress your feelings and they will magically disappear. Some incidents may require more healing time than others, and that is to be expected. If you feel that you are ready to let go, but still have more to work through with an issue, listen to your instinct. Talk to someone about it; this can be someone close to you or a professional. Write things down. Journaling each night can help you on the healing process. Use creativity to express yourself. Taking on a new hobby and channeling your energy towards a situation into it can be helpful and also fun. Once you are in a place of tolerance, you are ready to let the issue go.

Observing animals can be a great lesson. Have you ever observed how cats can get into small fights? For whatever reason, they will paw each other in the face a few good times and then it will be over. The cats will just go right back to whatever they were doing like it never even happened. It is very different from us humans who can hold onto things for even years at a time.

The way that you approach these negative situations can be telling of how easily you are going to be able to let them go. Claim your responsibility and acknowledge what part of the problem that you contributed to. Blaming others can be a release of anger, but this will not get down to the root of the issue. Once you have identified your role, think about the role of the other person. Do not put any more anger or resentment into the thought, simply think about how they contributed. Now, switch gears entirely—think about the present. Think about where you are in life and what you strive for; do the same with the other person involved. Keep in mind how you want to live a happier life, a fulfilling life. If the other person means something to you in the present moment, your relationship is more valuable than whatever problem you are trying to let go of. Let yourself forgive them and recognize that this past mistake does not define any future interaction. You do not have to inform them that you have forgiven them, and this is where the personal growth comes into play. Being able to do something on your own accord without the approval or recognition of others shows how secure and balanced you are as a person. You can, of course, start a conversation if you feel that it is the right thing to do. Mending the relationship can come in time when you feel that both parties are ready.

Everyone is a flawed human – that means everyone will also make mistakes for the rest of their lives. It doesn't matter who it is, they will make a mistake at some point. It only makes sense to forgive others if we want to be forgiven ourselves. You may say, well that person made an even larger mistake than I would ever make. Can we really compare someone else's ignorance to our own? Is that really an equal playing field?

Forgiving yourself may almost be harder than forgiving someone else. If you have gotten far along on your journey of knowing yourself, then it is going to be easier to hold resentment for inside. To cope with this, imagine viewing the situation as a bystander. Viewing things from a third party perspective can allow you to see the entire picture. This will ensure that you are not too harsh with yourself while you work on forgiveness. Think about what you stand for: your morals and your values. Don't be afraid to identify those moments when you broke from those characteristics that you find most important. Just like forgiving someone else, you may need to work through your anger and feelings. Know that you cannot do anything differently, no matter how much you wish that things were different. The past is set in stone, but the future is where your opportunity for bettering yourself lies. It is never too late to start from day 1, almost as if you are pressing a reset button and putting your best self forward.

Happiness exists deeper than what appears on the surface. Remember, you need to include your entire being as you work to achieve happiness. Having a healthy mind, physical body, and emotional self is going to ensure that you can keep balanced. By ignoring your struggles, you may appear happy to others, but might still be missing some of the essential healing that needs to take place within. Being a happy person means being a well-rounded person, capable of handling life and all that comes along with it. Knowing how to make yourself happy is the root that starts the process of going for other things in life that create happiness. With this strong foundation, you will be amazed at the great things to follow.

In all of the challenging situations that you encounter, viewing life with a glass half full mentality will transform your situation before your eyes. Your daily decisions will become smarter, and your outlook on life will appear more optimistic. Letting go of the weight of negativity is a beautiful feeling, one that we all deserve to experience. This positive viewpoint is the key to creating happiness daily. Remember, it is your choice to put yourself forward with positive energy. If you ever have a challenging moment, stop for a minute and think about one way that you can approach it with positivity. Practice is what it takes to be naturally optimistic, and with an open mind, your possibilities will be endless. Choosing to live

with a more positive demeanor is going to open up more doors

for you in the future, ones that you may have not noticed

otherwise.

Chapter 7 - Break the Boundaries

For personal advancement, challenging yourself is a must. In order to expand your mind to include more happiness, you have to be willing to step outside of your comfort zone. A task that is easier said than done, nobody likes to intentionally be put into an uncomfortable situation. As people, we like to stick to what we know. If something is familiar and safe, we tend to gravitate towards it. This can include situations and even people in our lives, so choosing your surroundings carefully in every respect is important. When you find that it is hard to generate your own happiness, the environment around you could easily be a part of what is weighing you down. If you are not ready for a total life overhaul, try starting on a smaller scale. Getting out of town for the weekend or even starting a new hobby and joining a group for it can break up the mundane. In any situation where you will potentially learn something new and meet someone new, you will be positively challenging your boundaries.

In retrospect, a fleeting moment of being nervous or uncomfortable is not comparable to the long-lasting happiness and personal growth that you can achieve by simply pushing yourself a little bit harder. Take chances, and use your newfound self-confidence to propel you forward! You do not have to set forth alone; doing something new with a friend can be dually beneficial, both for self-improvement and also for your friendship. Bonding over something new and challenging is a great way to become closer friends. Having a motivator is going to allow you to push yourself even farther than you might if you were alone. Having the ability to reflect on your struggles with someone who understands them completely is also going to be very beneficial to you. Make a plan with you friend to explore something new. This can be anything from a dance class to a weekly road trip to visit more places in your hometown. By turning this into a plan, you will feel much more motivated to try new things and break all of the barriers of your comfort zone.

Anxiety is an inevitable feeling, the one that pushes our limits of comfort. Having a healthy level of it has been scientifically proven to help us perform our best. It is often overlooked that anxiety is a normal reaction to situations in life. The kind of anxiety that arises to help us recognize that a situation is outside of our comfort zone is important to self-growth. Of course, too much of this is going to hinder you. Being able to keep your fears at bay while still feeling nervous is healthy and normal. Experiencing this sensation can almost act like an adrenaline rush, and learning to channel this energy into something that you can utilize is going to help you break down those barriers. Your anxiety levels rest on a curve, and if you want to use it to better yourself, you must really know your limits. It all becomes a process of trial and error. Test yourself in various situations and make mental notes about when you feel that you have been pushed too far. You will learn what your acceptable healthy level of nervousness is. (Source: Neel Burton MD)

Knowing how to cope with your anxiety is going to assist you in this process of transformation. If your boundaries get pushed too far, you must know how to be self-assuring and reel them back into place. Having a designated person you can talk to when your anxiety becomes a burden is very important. This can be anyone from a mental health professional to your best friend. Always set aside time during the week to do things that make you feel good. Spending time with yourself is just as important as spending time with a loved one. You are going to have to work on nurturing your relationship with yourself, building it up so it becomes strong and unwavering. A few more keys to preventing anxiety from getting to your head are getting enough sleep, drinking plenty of water, allowing yourself down time with no obligations, and participation in physical activities that stimulate your endorphins. With a combination of a few of these things (or all of them), you will be on the right track for keeping your anxiety in check.

Achieving ultimate satisfaction is always going to be hard work. If it were easy, everyone would always be happy and no life lessons would be learned. This is, unfortunately, not a realistic way of living. Life is going to be filled with ups and downs, the most unpredictable of situations. Ride the waves of happiness while you can and learn how to surf through the storms. Having a realistic approach is going to ensure that you are not disappointed or let down. Tell yourself that you are going to do your best no matter what, and you will find your own ways to cope when times get tough. Having a mentality of "this too shall pass" is going to act in a self-reassuring way. No situation is going to stay the same forever, so you should not let yourself be taken over with pessimism. Learn ways in which you can comfort yourself if you feel that you are getting into a dark place. What makes you feel good? Make a pack of self-care items that you can turn to when you just need a break from life and all that stresses you out. Remember to use positive words when referring to yourself and try to keep all of your thoughts on the same level of kindness. As you start to become anxious or stressed, your muscles might physically begin to tighten causing your whole body to become sore. Make sure that you pay attention to your physical health and utilize massages and warm baths when necessary. (Wolff, 2016)

Expanding your mind to see new choices might lead you to possibilities you never thought were realistic before. It is easy to get stuck in tunnel vision, only seeing one route to accomplish the task at hand. Broaden your viewpoint and you may find that there is more than one way to approach a situation. Finding this kind of inspiration is easier than you think. This is why the importance of trying new things is stressed, because being around others who are going through similar situations will benefit you. We all have our different ways of coping and accomplishing tasks. The best part is, there is no right way or wrong way. It is often true that there are multiple successful ways to take on any given situation; all will clearly yield different results. Think about the lasting impact that your choice will present, and you will be able to continue down your path of success.

With anything, it is impossible to know it if you haven't felt it. This applies to traveling, interacting with others, learning, and more. Limiting yourself may seem safe and comfortable, and most times, you won't even realize you're doing it. Your comfort zone becomes your protective bubble, and this can be very hard to step outside of. Think about how much there is to potentially learn—you will have new experiences under your belt that might assist you with other moments in your life. When you work on improving your flexibility to change, you strengthen your ability to go with the flow. Everything is interconnected, often proving to be effortlessly woven together. Put yourself out there! If you need to brainstorm, get as comfortable as you can. Sit down in your favorite coffee shop and bring a pad of paper and a pen. Use this moment as a time of relaxation and watch how easily the ideas with begin to flow. If you associate this process with feelings of comfort, you will train yourself to be more accepting of change. Remember, it is never selfish to work on yourself. Becoming a happier person is not something to be ashamed of, and in fact, it should be talked about more frequently. If you do not hear the discussion, don't be afraid to create it!

Throughout your journey, you may realize that you don't know yourself as well as you'd like to. Be patient with yourself and any inflexibilities that you may be holding onto. This does not have to hinder you; you can use it as a stepping stone. Build your emotional strength up—realize that constructive criticism from others does not define you, nor do any negative remarks. By building up your backbone, you are putting yourself one step closer to deciding what parts of yourself that you personally want to work on. At the end of the day, your opinion is most important, after all. Keep the goal in mind, the goal of seeing things as a glass half full. Stray away from thoughts of wanting to impress or please other people. The only person that you should ever seek approval from is yourself. As it has been said, when you are happy with the person that you are at the end of the day, you will be able to focus on new opportunities rather than being insecure or uncomfortable.

If you have something to say, then say it! Silencing our voices is one of the easiest ways that we put limits on ourselves. This of course, applies to positive thoughts and optimistic words. In dealing with negativity, it should be channel out which pushes the positivity forward. If you see someone and wish to compliment them, don't hold back. Think about the impact you will have on that person's day and also the kindness it will bring to your soul. Being a selfless person is one of the most admirable traits to have. If you see something that you disagree with, think about the core reasons why. Use your voice to make your opinion known. The most powerful historic figures in our history books did not get to where they were by keeping quiet. You have the ability to change not only your life, but also, the lives of others on a large scale. Expressing yourself is a powerful feeling, one that we should all indulge upon. Especially if you are a particularly shy and reserved individual, create goals to speak up more often about things that matter to you.

Being able to listen to others speak up and remain neutral could prove to be challenging, especially if their opinion or belief clashes with your own. Getting into a healthy and intellectual debate is great for helping your brain expand and pushing yourself out of your comfort zone. Name calling and arguing is an example of a non-constructive way to use your voice. Refrain from being driven by negativity and think about how you can approach the situation differently. Keep your thoughts clear and express your points with supporting facts. Opinions should always be supported by facts and not other opinions. You will be respected for educating others while staying true to your stance. These tips can assist in almost any relationship or marriage. The art of arguing is one that is worth mastering.

If you take a look at some of the most successful dynamics between people, both platonic and romantic, you'll probably recognize that one of the key components is communication and lots of it. Being able to talk to someone and address a problem seems like it should be easy and natural, but it can be difficult for most. Nobody likes confrontation, but you do not necessarily need to take your discussion to an aggressive level. Talking as if you were having any other regular conversation is the best way to keep feelings neutral and negativity to a minimum. Express your points clearly, and do not hold any expectations to the conversation. This is the easiest way to remain unbiased and to keep your temper in check. When you are able to converse with someone about any topic, you will be able to be rational in your decisions and choice of words. We've all said things we don't mean out of anger, but this is hurtful and not going to help you make any progress.

Bottom line—experiencing discomfort is going to help you grow as a person and help you to reach your ultimate level of happiness. Relish in your new experiences and trust in the new friendships that you will acquire. Use your communication skills to have a healthy and successful relationship. Secure your focus and utilize it in your work life, helping you to be a valuable employee. The best part about learning how to be confident is that you will learn how to embrace almost any situation for exactly what it is. Seeing things for what they really are is a surefire way to make sure that your honesty and integrity are intact. All of this is very hard work, and that is no secret. This is something you are going to feel great about working towards, though. With hard work comes positive rewards, and you will be able to see your happiness evolving before your eyes. You will soon forget what it feels like to be uncomfortable because you will be transforming these instances into positive experiences.

As you are working on this challenge to see things in a more positive way, keep track of your progress. You can do this by simply journaling every week, or even every day if you feel up to it. This progress report will act as a timeline of growth that you can refer back to. There will always be down days in everyone's lives, but don't let them get the best of you.

Turn to your journal and see how amazing that you are doing and how you have accomplished so much. Don't forget to utilize the reward system to treat yourself as you accomplish milestones of progress. Through this process, others around you are bound to notice this happier and more positive you. As it has been stated, this energy is going to attract more positive things and people into your life. So, before you think "why me," instead think about what you can do to improve your situation. This is ultimately going to make you more resilient and accepting of change.

Chapter 8 - Beacon of Hope

When everything is falling apart, you can find solace in knowing that there is always a silver lining. This saying often used, but what can it mean for you? As you get farther and farther down the line of becoming a more positive person, your ability to see the bright side of things is going to improve tremendously. Although the silver lining is not always a tangible item, it is more of a representation of your optimism. When things are going downhill, it is important to look up. Keeping your head up keeps you strong when you need to deal with hard situations. If you are in a bad situation, and you cannot identify anything positive about it, take a step back. Think about your health, are you healthy? Are you thankful to have a roof over your head? Are you alive? Even though these aspects may not necessarily relate to the problem at hand, they are still things that you can be thankful for, your silver lining. Thinking this way will encourage your brain to turn to positive affirmations during hard situations rather than wallowing in the negative. This takes plenty of practice, and repetition is the only way to strengthen this skill. Think about what you are thankful for on a daily basis, even write these things down. By having them on paper, you will be able to refer to one the next time you need to are in need of some positive inspiration.

When presented with a situation that generates fear or discomfort, our fight or flight reaction kicks in. Do you want to work on combating this or do you want to turn the other way? Both options are perfectly natural reactions to have, and either can apply to your situation. No matter which route you decide to take, consider that you are going to experience a life lesson at the very least. Reflection on your choices, as discussed before, can help you to learn more about yourself and what you may have done differently. This reflection is going to assist you in the future if you are ever faced with a similar situation again. So, whether you decide that you want to approach a situation head-on, or if you'd rather leave it up to fate and remove yourself, you will be benefiting by gaining more knowledge. Use all of the techniques that you have learned thus far to help you in making your decision.

If you want to stay and "fight" during a situation, do not take this literally. Fighting does not mean using aggressive language or behavior to manipulate a situation to your liking. Remember, there are some things that you just cannot change. Instead, start the battle with your positive thinking to combat things when times are tough. Using the skills that you have learned to think positively, emit all of the good energy that you can towards a situation. You do not have to be religious to put out good intentions. By doing this, the pressure will be lifted from your shoulders and you should realize that you are trying your best. As tempting as it can be to fan the flames, you need to keep yourself in check to maintain that balance that you have been working so hard on. When you are explaining your situation to others, don't forget to use positive language as well. Explain the problem and follow up with an expression of hopefulness. Every step that you take counts towards the final result.

If you feel that you cannot muster up enough positive energy, it is okay to remove yourself from a situation to prevent a negative outcome. This should be not looked at as failure or fear, but simply as knowing what you need to do in order to get through it. Just because you turn your back on a situation does not necessarily mean that you are avoiding or suppressing it. You will often find that there is more than one way to approach a solution. By turning your back on what is expected of you, you'll be exercising your right to make responsible decisions that work best for you. It is not always the most conventional or obvious method that is going to help a situation. Experiment with the way that you choose to handle it. If you find that you've reached a dead end, you can always regroup and try again. Life works like a maze and the only way you are going to reach a solution is by trying different options.

By understanding the different ways that you can handle a bad situation, you will see that finding a silver lining is not that difficult. The basis of making the right choice comes from being sure of who you are as a person. Know where you stand on issues and know what your morals are. Remember that it is okay to feel overwhelmed when you are trying to seek positivity, because stress can affect you not only mentally, but physically as well. Fear produces certain hormones that actually activate your body's fight or flight reaction. These hormones release a big burst of energy that you can either utilize to tackle the problem head on, or store inside to give you the courage to move forward. The process is a full body experience, and you can always learn from it.

When you live life with an observant eye, you will notice opportunities that you wish you had a chance at partaking in. What stops you from going for them? Perhaps you feel that they are unattainable and beyond your reach. Maybe you are intimidated to put yourself out there because many others are also trying for the same thing. Whatever the reason, the solution is to train your brain to see every opportunity as one that you can accomplish. With every closed door comes a new path to an open one. A common mistake that is made is giving up too easily as soon the words "you can't" are heard. If you have ever been told that you can't do something, you probably know that defeated feeling and hold slight resentment for the one preaching this negativity. How can you prove to others that you are capable of great things when you believe in yourself but they do not believe in you? It takes a very strong person to defeat adversity.

To become the strongest version of yourself that you can be, it is essential to have the right mindset. Instead of feeling defeated when something seems impossible, look at it as a challenge instead. Decide that you are going to try your best to make it happen, to prove all of the doubters wrong. The silver lining mentality comes into play here and will assist you when you need some inspiration. Don't take no for an answer. As long as you are not causing pain or damage to anyone around you, keep persevering. Have a goal in mind to make those naysayers change their answer to yes. Banish all excuses from your vocabulary and your mentality. No more waiting around for the right time, the right time to do something extraordinary is always immediately. Have as much faith in yourself as you can and reflect on it daily. Nobody likes a person who cannot remain humble while still being successful. Use your reflection to remain grounded and level-headed. As you gain success along the way, use it to propel you forward into even more success.

Life can be painful at times, and nobody is immune to this pain. Bad things happen, some that even change us as people. Take all of the bad things that have happened to you and channel that strength that you used to get through them. As it has been mentioned, the past does not define you. Sure, there have been moments that have shaped you along the way, but you made it through to this moment right now. That factor alone is a huge silver lining and a cause for daily celebration. Talking about your hardships can be very beneficial, not only to remind you of what you have been through, but also to inspire those around you. It is possible that your voice can become the voice for many. When people experience adversity, they often feel very isolated and alone, as if no one else understands what they are going through. Sharing your struggles publically could benefit you by being able to discuss them, and also by inspiring others to keep on fighting.

If you need to gain a bit of perspective, consider that nothing is ever as negative as you think it is. Comparing your struggle to someone who is in a life or death situation, for example, is always an eye-opener. Not to invalidate anything that you are going through, but doing this to simply realize that you are lucky and you can push forward. Alternatively, you can also remind yourself that you have a powerful mind, one that can think of several different routes to get to the same finish line. Just because the outlook seems poor at the time does not mean that it cannot be changed or altered. By way of volunteer work, you will be able to put yourself into the shoes of those who are struggling. This may be beneficial to you along the way of your own journey. Also, reading memoirs is encouraged. Hearing other people's life stories will change the way you think about your own life and possibly provide you with the necessary inspiration that you require.

If you decide to pursue some volunteer work, you will be using your positive energy in one of the best ways possible. Happiness comes from helping others, and you will also have another skill to put onto your resume. Overall, there is no downside. As you lend a hand to helping others, you will feel happier and important to society. This can also strengthen your bond with your own community. Banding together to fight for the greater good is a very uplifting and unifying experience. Almost every organization could use the help of some volunteers. Think about some causes that are important to you, and do your research on which companies you would like to personally support. Whether you are on the road to starting college or already well established in your career, volunteering is a positive addition to your set of skills and can be utilized when needed. It can open your eyes to different struggles you may have not been aware of previously.

To have a purpose in life is going to solidify your desire to seek the silver lining. Defining your purpose can sound overwhelming and scary, but just remember that you do not need to stick to a single purpose. Perhaps you have just gotten out of a bad relationship and are learning how to stand on your own two feet again. Maybe your purpose is going to be transforming yourself into a strong, independent person with everything that you do. As you gain more and more life experience, things will fall into your lap that might shed some light on what your purpose could be in a given moment. Say that you fulfill the task of becoming independent and then you have children in the future. Your purpose may shift to acting as the best mother and role model to those children that you can be. We are chameleons, always shifting to better adjust to the environment that we are given. If you are uninspired and do not know what to make your purpose, try starting out with becoming the happiest person that you can be. Work on doing something daily that will contribute to your happiness, avoid those things that are meant to drag you down.

The key is to dedicate yourself to something, whether that be a craft, a person, or even yourself. Consume your mind with thoughts about how to better reach your goals and you will soon realize that you have a new purpose. Being dedicated is a trait that all successful people share. Without this, it becomes easier to give up and cast aside your aspirations. Passion is also essential. Keep your passion alive by changing things up when they begin to feel stale. Do your research and learn as much as you possibly can; education is power. When you begin your journey, pay attention to who you are surrounding yourself with. If you find that you have people in your life that are unsupportive of what you are aspiring to do, maybe reconsider the value of their friendship or relationship. Many patterns and methods are repeated here, all reaching towards the same common goals of happiness, positivity, and success.

How to let go of a friend that has become toxic and is draining you of positivity? There are multiple ways to go about it, and it may be best to choose which you think would work best. One way is to slowly back away from that person.

That means to get busier and hang out with them less and less,

and make it seem as natural as possible. Another way that

may work better for friendships that lasted a long time is to

just talk it out with the person as objectively as possible. Make

sure that you tell them that you respect the friendship that you

have had, but you need to space due to whatever happened.

Say that you know they are a good friend so they will

understand. Letting go of a relationship is never easy, but

sometimes it can be for the best.

Many people use landmark dates to decide that they

want to change their lives, for example, New Year's Day.

During this time, people make resolutions to be better and to

do better in the year to come. While this is a great goal to

have, do not limit yourself to changing only at the start of a

new year. Any day can be "day 1." If you wake up one morning

feeling inspired, take initiative! Putting your plan into action

immediately will ensure that you do not miss out on any

opportunities that you might have if you delay. Always

remember that you are in control of your own life. You can make changes at any time and you can completely transform your lifestyle at the drop of a hat. Once you stop fear from holding you back, you will feel invincible. Think about all of the things that you have wanted to try but haven't yet because of irrelevant excuses. By checking one off of your list, you are going to feel a huge surge of accomplishment.

Chapter 9 - The Importance of Kindness

While much of the quest for happiness and positivity is focused on self-improvement, there is also an importance that should be focused on the way that you treat others around you. If you are living your daily life and casting negativity towards other people, it is likely going to hinder your overall happiness and progress. Think about the way that a negative interaction would impact your day if you were on the receiving end. There is a way that a lack of kindness can feel like a lack of empathy. You probably wouldn't want to befriend the other person after your interaction, nor would you feel like you have good energy inside to contribute to the day ahead. Always treat others in a way that you would expect to be treated yourself. This is a lesson that you have probably been taught from a young age, and it still applies the older that you get in life. As a bigger picture, the more kindness that is spread into the world, the more happiness we will experience collectively. The act of being kind is contagious, so don't be afraid to express yourself often.

Being nice to other people feels good. If you are ever feeling down, try reaching out to someone and doing something nice with no prompt or expectations. Chances are, their reaction will make you feel a lot better. When you decide to do something nice from the bottom of your heart, you should not expect to receive the exact same level of kindness back. Of course, this is ideal, but being truly selfless gets rid of the expectations to receive something after you give it. As humans, we thrive on positive and healthy social interaction. While some of us more than others enjoy being social, when the opportunity presents itself, experiencing someone who is kind is going to feel uplifting. This phenomenon occurs because being kind actually releases endorphins just like exercising does. As we have learned, endorphins can work wonders in making sure that you stay balanced and happy in life. As you keep making the choice to be kind, your heart will become softer, and you will be able to see the beauty in things that maybe once you didn't feel so positively about. Overall, kindness is one of the most underrated traits that a person can have.

Another benefit to choosing kindness is that others who witness your actions will be impacted. Being nice can impact your friends, family, and even total strangers. Learning by example is one of the easiest ways to form a habit, so be aware of the message that you are sending out. What we see around us daily has the ability to influence us, so think about what your daily impact on others is. Do you feel that you benefit society with the actions that you choose? With the thought in mind to do something kind at least once per day, you can improve your social presence. Choosing kindness breeds tolerance and creates understanding. When people are treated well, there is less of a divide, even when there is a difference of opinion. Kindness is one of those traits that has the capability to unite people. Banding together for the greater good is one of the most selfless things that you can choose to do, and it has been proven time and time again in history to be successful.

If you see someone broken down on the side of the road and you own a pair of jumper cables, pull over to help them. If you notice someone struggling at the grocery store with a handful of bags, offer to walk them to their car and carry some of their load. In today's world, we sometimes have the mentality to keep to ourselves and turn a blind eye at all times. There are many cases when getting involved could make a great impact, though. Use your judgement wisely and try to break down some of those barriers that people unintentional put up on a daily basis. However, do not be discouraged if someone declines your good deed. The importance of recognizing boundaries is as equally important as being kind. For reasons unknown to you, other people might steer clear of your gestures, and that is okay. Each opportunity to interact with someone becomes a learning experience.

When it comes to possessions and material items, make sure that you are not allowing them to rule you. It feels good to live comfortably, to have all of the things that you want and need. Owning a lot of nice material things can bring you a sense of temporary bliss, not to be confused with true long-lasting happiness. Balance is also essential in this case, though. Those who become obsessed with collecting material items might lose track of reality and what is actually essential for living. With this disconnect, there may be times when it is harder to see others as peers instead of competition. Choosing this path is unhealthy for many reasons and might only provide you with a facade of happiness. If you were to think about your life stripped of all possessions, would you be able to still be happy on your own?

A striking example of a wonderful humanitarian is Mother Teresa. As a nun, she devoted herself to helping others, in particular, the poor and the sick. During a train ride in the late 40's, she experienced what she believed was the realization of her life's purpose. She decided to take a voyage to India in order to fulfil this newfound purpose. There she made it her mission to assist those within Calcutta's slums. She opened a school, created housing for the dying, and even convinced the local government to allow her funding for these projects. As time progressed, her good hearted nature did not slow down. She went on to open an orphanage, several mobile health clinics, a nursing home, and a community for lepers. Her efforts were not only limited to Calcutta. By the time a couple decades had passed, she had impacted up to 123 countries all around the world. She is a prime example of why it is so important to spread kindness and positivity at every chance that you get. What she did for people is still widely recognized and will always be recognized, making her a true inspiration for all. (Dunigan, 2007)

Channeling inspiration from a public figure like Mother Teresa, or even just from someone in your life who is a positive role model, can be conclusive to you realizing your own purpose. If you do not know where to begin, learn by example. There is endless literature on positive influences from every era and every geographic location. Learning about the struggles that they faced at the time and why they were inspired to make a difference just might help you to do the same in this present time. Think about what you wish that you could change about the world and brainstorm ways that you might be able to make an impact. Donating to charities is a great way to support a cause when you are unsure of how to reach out on your own. Another way is to volunteer, as was previously mentioned. Volunteer work is utilizing your kindness and manifesting it as much as you possibly can.

Think about what issues you feel most passionate about. Maybe you'd like to assist the homeless, help stray animals, or work with children. Start a discussion with your friends and family; this might provide you with more insight in the direction that you should take as well as the potential for them to get involved as well. Through volunteer work, you may find that you will have the opportunity to travel. Take this experience if it becomes an option for you. In your volunteering, you are going to learn a lot and be exposed to many things you may not have known before. If you don't see an organization that represents the cause that you want to fight for, take action! You can start your own non-profit or even simply set up a donation page to put funding towards the issues that you care about most. Getting involved is one of the best ways to become the most selfless person that you can be. Volunteer work is altruistic, and always full of lessons to be learned.

If you're not helping others, there is a chance you might be hurting others. This is nothing to beat yourself up over, as we have all done this before. Being able to recognize that you are doing something unhealthy in relation to another person is super important, though. One of the most common ways that we hurt others is through our words. When you have a lot of anger surging through you, it is easier to say things that you may not necessarily mean. During the most heated arguments is usually when people get their feelings hurt by unnecessary flying words. This comes from not being able to express ourselves clearly and separate our thoughts from our emotions. When you allow this type of behavior, you will often feel guilt later on down the road. Once your temper subsides and you are left with only the true facts about the situation, you may realize the ways in which you were wrong. Learn from this, and try not to let arguments progress to that level in the future.

Another way that we may accidentally hurt someone is through the course of our actions. Similar to expressing yourself through words you may not mean, when you are experiencing negative emotions, it becomes likely to take action out of anger. This often results in the same feelings of guilt and regret. Think hard before you make your choices, because your actions could have a greater impact that you realize. Through the process of getting to know yourself better, you will find ways that you can calm yourself down in order to prevent escalation. Remember, you are likely feeling negativity about the situation, so do your best to not take it out on the other person. Being able to express yourself clearly is going to bring you to a solution much faster than taking your negativity out on another person.

The more that you are able to be harmonious amongst others, the more connected you will feel socially. We all have our moods when we would rather just spend time alone at home, but when it comes to social interaction, being able to have good experiences with it comes from having refined social skills. By utilizing all of the different methods of kindness, from volunteering to simply doing something kind for a loved one, you will feel a bigger sense of community and support in turn. Being connected to others leads to happiness and positivity. At any opportunity that you get, take the time to see your friends and family. Let them know how much you care and be open and honest with them. By doing this, it encourages others to reach out to you as well.

Chapter 10 - On the Whole

Happiness and positivity does not only stem from one person, place, or thing. The process begins with the exploration and understanding of your own mind. Think about why you do the things that you do, what you can help and what is simply your brain chemistry. Being able to identify and separate your thoughts and emotions will leave you with the most level-headed mind.

Learn how to believe in yourself and how to spread self-confidence into the things that you try to accomplish daily. Being supportive of yourself is ultimately one of the most important steps for personal growth. Setting goals is also encouraged, because it will allow for some healthy challenge and motivation to take place. In order to experience new happiness, you must be willing to push yourself out of your comfort zone. Trying new things may be scary at first, but you will be glad that you did. As you face your daily tasks, learn how to view every situation in the most positive light possible.

Seeing the silver lining in all situations is going to help you stay out of any ruts or slumps in life because you will feel like you are able to push through them. Once you learn how to treat yourself kindly, do not forget to extend your kindness to others around you as well. Radiating kindness is a great way to generate more positivity into your life. Incorporating all of these elements into your life is going to keep you balanced and well-rounded.

Nothing great comes easy, so do not become discouraged if you struggle from time to time. This is a normal part of life, and it is only human to make mistakes. Wake up each day deciding that you are going to be the best version of yourself that you can be, and happiness and positivity is sure to follow.

Bibliography

Axe, Josh. "7 Ways to Hack Your Biology to Manufacture More Natural "Feel-Good" Chemicals." *Dr. Axe.* Food Is Medicine, 22 June 2017. Web.

Barker, Eric. "Neuroscience Reveals 4 Rituals That Will Make You Happy." *FEATURE Neuroscience Reveals 4 Rituals That Will Make You Happy.* Barking Up The Wrong Tree, 28 Feb. 2016. Web.

Bergland, Christopher. "The Neurochemicals of Happiness." *Psychology Today.* Sussex Publishers, 29 Nov. 2012. Web.

Burton, Neel. "Can Anxiety Be Good for Us? " Psychology Today. Sussex Publishers, 15 July 2012. Web.

Dunigan, Brian. "Mother Teresa " *Encyclopædia Britannica.* Encyclopædia Britannica, Inc, 07 Sept. 2007. Web.

Hacheyart, Norman, Liam Ofarrell, Jesus, Olufunmi, Dave, Arina Nikitina, Ashley (Reining in Mom), and Cynthia. "Long Term Goals: How To Create And Achieve Your Long Term Goal."*Goal Setting Guide.* N. p. , 17 Feb. 2012. Web.

Wallis, Claudia. "The New Science of Happiness." *Time.* Time Inc. , 09 Jan. 2005. Web.
Wolff, Carina. "11 Habits Of Calm People That Keep Them Relaxed & In Control Of Their Emotions. " *Bustle.* Bustle, 10 Nov. 2016. Web.

Yates, Diana. "Study: Happiness Improves Health and Lengthens Life " *News Bureau.* N. p. , 01 Mar. 2011. Web.

One Last Thing...

If you enjoyed this book or found it useful, I'd be very grateful if you'd post a short review on Amazon. Your support really does make a difference and I read all the reviews personally so I can get your feedback and make this book even better.

When you give a rating, and write a short review on Amazon more people will get the benefit from this book.

Thanks again for your support! :)

sunlight
exercise.
laughter

foods

a newfound hobby to give
sense of accomplishment

try to do something productive

Self Recognition (Being your
own
cheerleader

Made in United States
Orlando, FL
13 February 2022